MANY HANDS COOKING

An International Cookbook for Girls and Boys

COOKED AND WRITTEN BY

TERRY TOUFF COOPER

AND

MARILYN RATNER

ILLUSTRATED BY *TONY CHEN*

Thomas Y. Crowell Company in cooperation with
the U.S. Committee for UNICEF   New York

Text copyright © 1974 by Terry Touff Cooper and Marilyn Ratner.
Illustrations copyright © 1974 by Tony Chen.
All rights reserved. Manufactured in the United States of America.
ISBN 0-690-00536-9   L.C. Card 74-11871
3   4   5   6   7   8   9   10

To the Tasters, D.C. and M.R.

A NOTE TO YOUNG COOKS

From Canada to China, from Belgium to Brazil, people are cooking delicious foods. You can, too. MANY HANDS COOKING has savory recipes from forty different lands. Among them you'll find old favorites, such as Sugar Crisps from England, and new tastes to be enjoyed, such as Groundnut Soup from Nigeria.

Each recipe is marked with a code. One hand means very simple to make. Three hands takes a little extra time and work. The rest of the recipes are in between— two hands, naturally.

Before you start to cook, get to know the design of this book. The first pages list definitions of cooking terms and kitchen tools to know. If you don't understand a word or a step in a recipe, check these pages. There are also hints on ingredients, safety, and measurements.

Recipes follow, taking you around the world. At first glance some of them may seem to be upside down, but you'll find that this arrangement allows you to stand the book up for easy recipe reading while you're cooking.

At the end of the book are international menu ideas for meals and parties. Another page describes CSM (a high-protein food) and gives two recipes for using it. And an index on the last page helps you to find your way to whatever recipe has caught your eye.

On many pages you'll notice most of the people are wearing their national costumes. These costumes are a beautiful part of a country's culture and history. Of course, in most countries today, these clothes are worn only for holidays and special events.

The recipes have been written so that they will be practical for U.S. cooks and kitchens. Try the recipes our way. Then you may want to make changes to suit your own taste. After all, that's how new recipes happen.

Let your eyes, your taste, and your hands take you on an exciting trip around the world.

Each numbered country on the map matches the page number of a country (and a recipe) listed below on the Contents page—for example 1 is Canada, 5 is Haiti, 35 is Turkey, and so forth.

CONTENTS

YOU BE THE JUDGE. Each recipe has a code.
⚜ (one hand) recipes are the easiest to make.
⚜⚜ (two hands) recipes are easy to make.
⚜⚜⚜ (three hands) recipes are not hard, but do take a little extra time and work.
If you've never cooked before, start with a one-hand recipe. You'll soon find that you can easily make even those rated by three hands. If you can follow directions, you can learn to cook anything.

SAFETY FIRST

Always use a pot holder or oven mitts in handling any hot pots or pans.

Ask someone older to help you to light the oven or stove—until you have learned how to do it safely yourself.

Keep the handles of any pots or pans cooking on the stove turned inward. That way you won't knock over hot food by accident.

Always pick up a knife by its handle, not by its blade.

When you've finished cooking, make sure all oven and stove dials are turned OFF.

GETTING STARTED

Whether or not you've cooked before, these tips will help you tackle a recipe.

1. Read the recipe from start to finish and see if you have everything you need.
2. Make a shopping list.
3. Buy the needed ingredients.
4. Wash your hands before handling food.
5. Get out all the ingredients and put them near your work space.
6. Gather the cooking equipment you need.
7. Read the recipe again. Look up any cooking terms you aren't sure of on pages xi–xiii.
8. For best results, always follow the recipe exactly at first. After that, you can try variations.
9. If you have a kitchen timer, use it. Then you'll be sure to bake or cook your food the right length of time.
10. *Have fun!*

A WORD ABOUT INGREDIENTS

Most of the ingredients used in these recipes are available at the supermarket. In a few cases a trip to a specialty grocery or gourmet food shop might be necessary and fun. If you can't find an ingredient, study the recipe and see if it can be left out. If not, maybe a substitute ingredient would do.

Brown rice is more nutritious than white rice, and some people prefer to use it. You can substitute it for white rice in these recipes. Be sure to check the cooking time on the brown rice package. Brown rice usually takes longer to cook than white rice, so allow for the extra time when you're using it in a recipe.

Margarine can be substituted for butter.

Plantains are sometimes referred to as cooking bananas. They are coarser than yellow eating bananas and aren't eaten raw. They aren't good uncooked. You can use green or yellow plantains in stews and soups. They should be almost brown before they are used in desserts.

Bean curd is made from soybeans. (Read the Tofu Toss recipe on page 44 for more about bean curd.) If you can't find bean curd in any store near your home, go to your local public library and look in the back of a Chinese or Japanese cookbook. You'll probably find the names and address of several mail-order food companies that sell bean curd listed there.

Eggs

To hard-cook eggs. Put the eggs into a saucepan with enough cold water to cover them. Heat the water until it boils. Turn off the heat. Cover the saucepan, and let the eggs stand in the hot water for 15 minutes. Drain off the water and cool the eggs at once by running cold water over them.

To separate eggs. Have two bowls, one for the yolks, the other for the whites. Crack open the egg by hitting it in the center against the hard edge of a bowl. Gently pull the shell apart and let the white drop into the bowl, keeping the yolk back in one half of the shell. Gently pour the yolk back and forth from one half of the eggshell to the other to free all the white from the yolk. Then drop the yolk alone into the other bowl.

To beat egg whites. Use a large bowl because the amount of egg white will expand. Make sure that both the bowl and the beater are very clean and dry. Put the egg whites into the bowl. With an egg beater or a wire whisk, beat the whites until they stand in stiff peaks when the beater is lifted from the bowl. The tops of the peaks should droop slightly for egg whites beaten stiff and should stand straight for egg whites beaten *very* stiff.

HANDY COOKING TOOLS

For Preparing Food

set of measuring cups in the following sizes: ¼ cup, ⅓ cup, ½ cup, 1 cup

set of measuring spoons: ⅛ t., ¼ t., ½ t., 1 t., 1 T.

mixing bowls: small, medium, and large

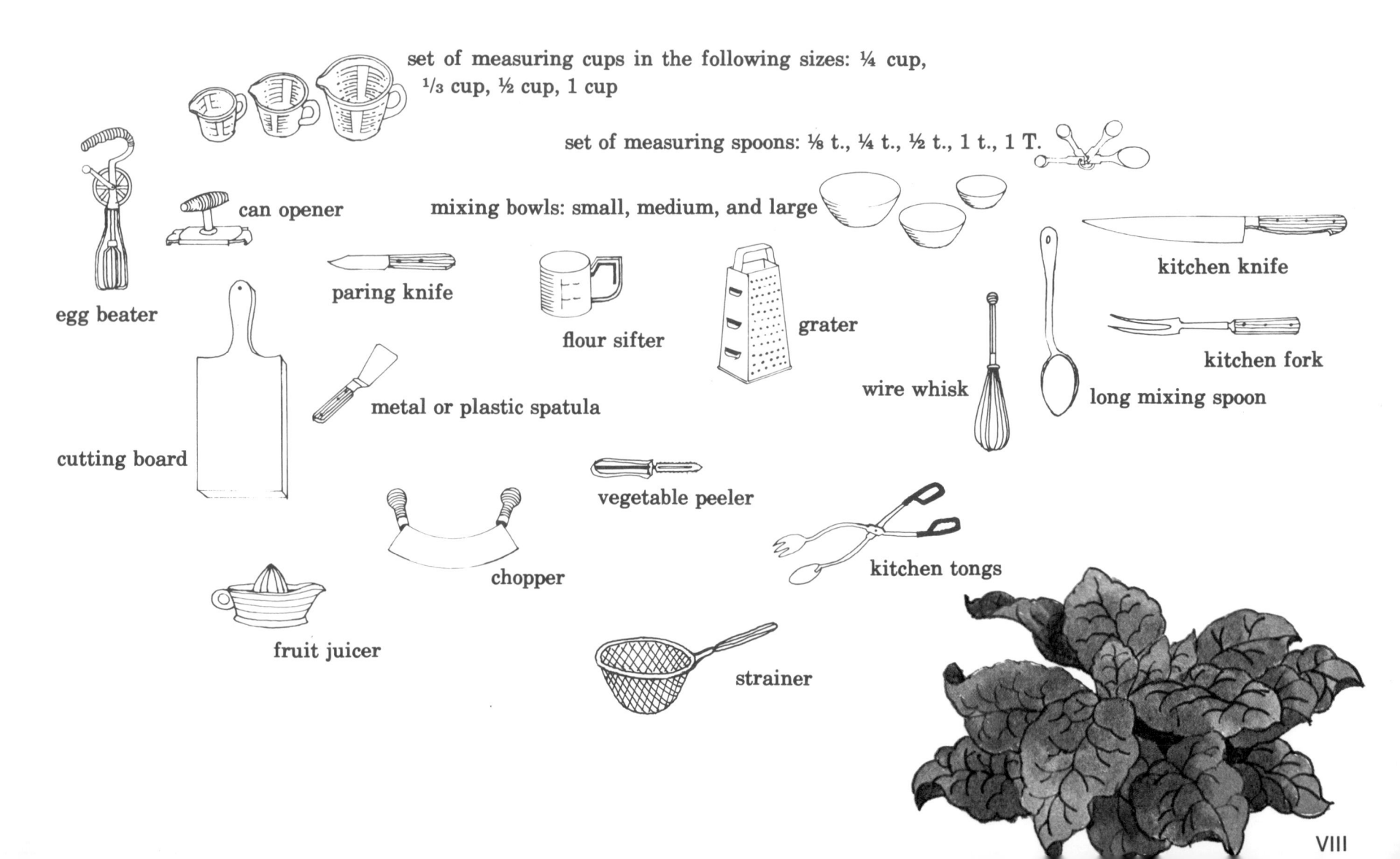

egg beater

can opener

paring knife

flour sifter

grater

kitchen knife

wire whisk

long mixing spoon

kitchen fork

cutting board

metal or plastic spatula

vegetable peeler

kitchen tongs

chopper

fruit juicer

strainer

For Cooking

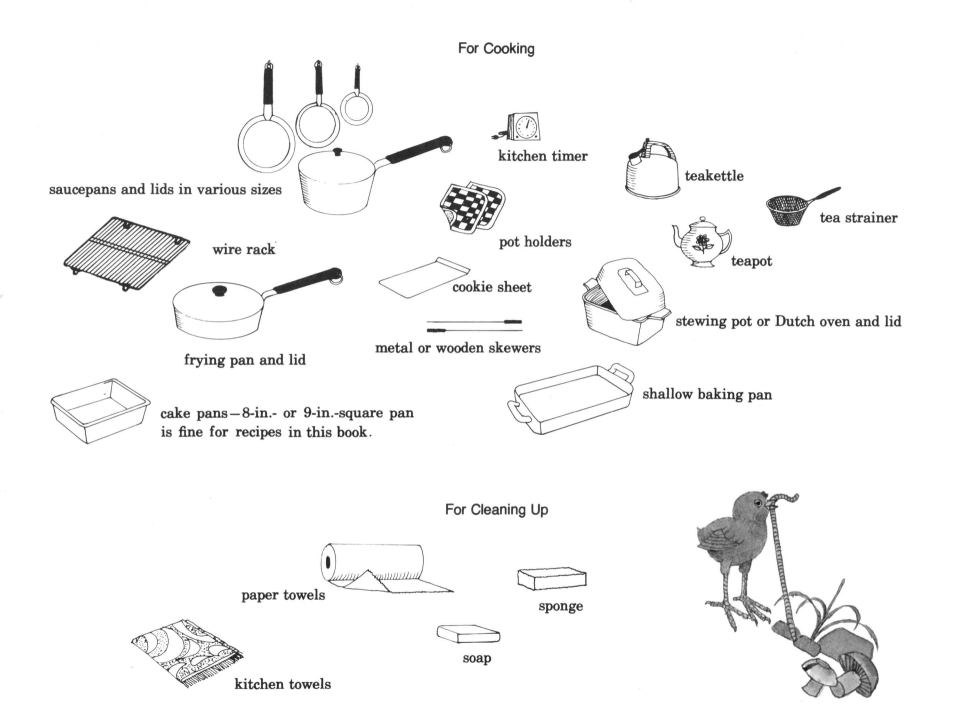

saucepans and lids in various sizes

kitchen timer

teakettle

tea strainer

wire rack

pot holders

teapot

cookie sheet

frying pan and lid

metal or wooden skewers

stewing pot or Dutch oven and lid

cake pans—8-in.- or 9-in.-square pan is fine for recipes in this book.

shallow baking pan

For Cleaning Up

paper towels

sponge

soap

kitchen towels

MEASURING MADE SIMPLE

To measure dry ingredients—flour, sugar, etc. Fill the right-sized measuring cup or spoon until it overflows. Then pull a straight-edged knife across the top to level off.

To measure liquids in a cup—milk, water, etc. Set measuring cup on a flat surface. Pour in liquid until full or fill to desired mark.

    in a spoon—vanilla, etc. Pour liquid into right-sized measuring spoon until full.

Measuring butter. One stick or ¼ lb. of butter is equal to ½ cup or 8 tablespoons. Half a stick equals ¼ cup or 4 tablespoons. To measure 2 tablespoons, cut off one quarter of a ¼-pound stick.

Abbreviations Used in the Recipes

in.	=	inch
lb.	=	pound
oz.	=	ounce
pkg.	=	package
pt.	=	pint
qt.	=	quart
T.	=	tablespoon
t.	=	teaspoon

Table of Measures

dash = less than ⅛ teaspoon, 1 shake of salt, pepper, or other seasoning

pinch = amount you can pick up between tip of a finger and thumb

3 teaspoons = 1 tablespoon
4 tablespoons = ¼ cup
8 tablespoons = ½ cup
1 cup = ½ pint or 8 ounces
2 cups = 1 pint or 16 ounces
16 ounces = 1 pound
4 cups = 2 pints or 1 quart
4 quarts = 1 gallon

KITCHEN TERMS TO KNOW

BAKE. To cook in an oven.

BATTER. An uncooked mixture of flour, liquid, and other ingredients, as for a cake or pancakes.

BEAT. To make foods smooth or light by stirring with an over-and-over motion. Usually done with a mixing spoon. For directions for beating egg whites until they are stiff see the paragraph under Eggs on page vii.

BLEND. To mix thoroughly two or more ingredients, usually with a spoon.

BOIL. To cook on top of the stove at a point where large bubbles come to the surface and break. To heat liquid to this point is to bring to a boil.

BROIL. To cook under or over direct heat—under a stove's broiler or over an open fire or grill.

BROWN. To cook until brown in color.

CHILL. To cool in the refrigerator.

CHOP. To cut up into small pieces with an up-and-down motion, using a knife or chopper. To chop into finer pieces is to mince.

COMBINE. To mix ingredients together.

COOL. To let hot food stand until it feels cool.

CRUMBLE. To break into small pieces with your hands.

CRUSH. To pound into small pieces.

CUBE. To cut into small blocks, from ½ in. by ½ in. to 1 in. by 1 in. in size.

DASH. Less than ⅛ t. of a dry ingredient.

DECORATE. To dress up a dish by using nuts, parsley, olives, etc.

DICE. To cut into small cubes less than ½ in. in size.

DRAIN. To pour off liquid.

FLOUR. (1) to roll food in flour. (2) to sprinkle a greased baking pan with a little flour; then shake until the flour lightly covers the pan. Pour off any extra flour.

FLAKE. To break into small pieces with a fork.

FLUFF. To lift gently with a fork so that pieces separate.

FOLD. To mix gently by lifting from bottom to top, then folding over.

GRATE. To rub food against a grater, so that it breaks into small pieces. Watch your knuckles!

GREASE. To smear a baking pan with a small amount of butter or shortening. Use clean fingers or a crumpled piece of waxed paper.

MARINATE. To soak in liquid.

MASH. To squash with the back of a fork or spoon until soft and smooth.

MEASURE. To put the amount called for in a recipe into a measuring cup or spoon.

MELT. To heat a solid food, such as butter or chocolate, until it turns liquid.

MINCE. To cut into pieces finer than chopped. Use the same motion as for chopping but do it for a longer time.

MIX. To stir ingredients together, usually with a spoon.

MIXTURE. A combination of ingredients.

PEEL. To strip off the outer layer or skin. Use hands for bananas and oranges; a paring knife for cucumbers and avocados.

PINCH. The amount you can hold between your thumb and first finger.

PREHEAT. To heat the oven to the temperature called for in the recipe before putting the food in to roast or bake.

SAUTÉ. To cook on top of the stove in a small amount of fat.

SEPARATE. Read the paragraph about Eggs on page vii.

SHRED. To cut or grate into long thin strips.

SIFT. To put dry ingredients, such as flour, through a sifter or strainer.

SIMMER. To cook gently on top of the stove just below the boiling point. Small bubbles appear around the edge of the liquid, but the surface moves only slightly.

SLICE. To cut into thin pieces with a knife.

SOFTEN. To leave butter or cream cheese at room temperature for 15 to 30 minutes, so that it becomes soft and easy to use.

SPRINKLE. To scatter on top of another food.

STEEP. To let stand in hot liquid.

STIR. To move around and around with a spoon.

THAW. To leave frozen food at room temperature so that it unfreezes.

TOAST. To brown and dry surfaces of food such as bread or seeds.

TOOTHPICK TEST. To insert a toothpick into cake or bread while it is baking to test doneness. Stick the toothpick into the middle. If it comes out clean—without crumbs or batter—the cake is done.

TOSS. To mix together by lifting and turning.

WEDGE. A pie-shaped piece of food, such as a quartered tomato.

WHIP. To beat rapidly such foods as eggs or cream, so that they become mixed with air, thicken, and expand.

CANADA

MAPLE SNOW
Serves 4 ♟

In the center of Canada's flag is a red maple leaf—a symbol of Canada's many maple trees. No wonder everyone likes to turn out in the early spring to help collect the sweet liquid from the sugar maples. The snow is still on the ground. The sap is gathered and boiled down into maple syrup. As a special treat, the hot syrup is poured over fresh snow. With cider and doughnuts, cups of sweet Maple Snow make festive refreshments at a sugaring-off party.

NOTE: You can use either pure maple syrup or maple-flavored syrup for this recipe.

INGREDIENTS

1 cup of clean snow or 1 tray of ice cubes
½ cup maple syrup

EQUIPMENT

pan or bowl
measuring cup
saucepan

4 small paper cups
tablespoon

HOW TO MAKE:

1. Fill a pan with snow. Be sure it is clean. Have all your ingredients ready before you bring in the snow, so it doesn't have time to melt. If there isn't any snow, make crushed ice. An easy way to do this is to wrap a few cubes of ice at a time in a kitchen towel and pound them with a heavy object, such as a rolling pin. Put the crushed ice in a bowl. Continue until all the cubes are crushed.
2. Heat the maple syrup in the saucepan over low heat for about two minutes until it is warm. Remove it from the heat.
3. Fill each paper cup with enough snow or ice to make a rounded top.
4. Drop a tablespoon or more of maple syrup on top of the snow or ice.

1

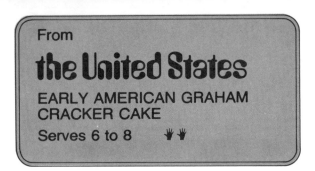

From
the United States

EARLY AMERICAN GRAHAM
CRACKER CAKE

Serves 6 to 8

Thanks to Dr. Sylvester Graham, you can bake this crunchy cake from crackers named after him. Graham, who lived in the early 1800's, insisted that whole wheat flour was far more healthy than white flour.

In *those* days, it was. Whole wheat flour was made by grinding the whole grain of wheat. For white flour, only the soft inside of the grain was used. The outer layers, rich with vitamins and minerals, were left out.

Today, white flour is "enriched" with the needed vitamins and minerals. But whole wheat flour is still naturally healthy. So are graham crackers, made from this flour. Use them for this one-bowl cake. It's all American.

INGREDIENTS

1¾	cup graham cracker crumbs (about 40 crackers)	½	cup shelled walnuts
⅓	cup unsifted flour	½	cup soft butter
2	t. baking powder	2	eggs
1	cup sugar	1	cup milk
½	cup shelled almonds	1	t. vanilla
		1	or 2 t. butter
		1	T. flour

EQUIPMENT

measuring cups
medium mixing bowl
measuring spoons
mixing spoon

chopper or paring knife
8-in.-square cake pan

HOW TO MAKE:

1. Preheat the oven to 375°.
2. Crush the graham crackers with your hands until you have 1¾ cups coarse crumbs about the size of bread crumbs.
3. Put the cracker crumbs into the mixing bowl with the flour, baking powder, and sugar. Stir with the spoon until they are combined.
4. Chop the almonds and walnuts into small pieces.
5. Add the soft butter, eggs, milk, vanilla, and chopped nuts to the dry ingredients.
6. Stir the mixture well. Then beat the batter until it is well blended.
7. Grease the cake pan with the butter.
8. Sprinkle it with the tablespoon of flour and shake the pan until the bottom is evenly coated. Shake out any extra flour.
9. Pour the batter into the cake pan.
10. Bake the cake for 45 minutes. Test with a toothpick for doneness. (See page xiii.)
11. Remove the cake from the oven and let it cool slightly. Cut it into squares and serve warm.

TOPPING: You might want to sprinkle powdered sugar or spread whipped cream on top. (To make whipped cream, see page 26.)

From
PUERTO RICO
CITRUS POPS
Makes 12 or more pops

Oranges, lemons, and bananas grow easily in Puerto Rico's sunny tropical climate. These tropical fruits are used for many of the island's drinks and desserts. In Puerto Rico, fruit ices bring relief from the heat, but you'll find fresh Citrus Pops delicious in any climate.

INGREDIENTS

1   cup sugar
2   cups water
3   oranges

3   lemons
2   bananas

EQUIPMENT

measuring cup
medium saucepan
mixing spoon
paring knife
fruit juicer and bowl
   to catch the juice

medium mixing bowl
fork
empty ice tray with
   dividers
toothpicks
paper cups (optional)

HOW TO MAKE:

1. Measure the sugar and water into the saucepan and place it on the stove over medium heat.
2. Cook, stirring all the time, until the sugar dissolves (about 3 minutes).
3. Remove the saucepan from the stove and let the mixture cool for about 15 minutes.
4. Cut the oranges and lemons in half and squeeze the juice from them.
5. Peel the bananas and place them in the mixing bowl. Mash them with the fork.
6. Add the citrus juice to the mashed bananas. Mix well.
7. Pour the sugar-water mixture into the mixing bowl. Mix well.
8. Pour it into an ice tray and place it in the freezer.
9. Freezing time varies from freezer to freezer. After 30 minutes, see if the Pops are solid enough to hold a toothpick. When they are, put a toothpick in each section.
10. Return the tray to the freezer until the Pops are fully frozen—at least 2 hours.

NOTE: The mixture can also be poured into paper cups and frozen. That way no toothpicks are needed.

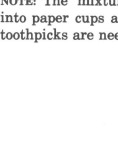

From

MEXICO

GUACAMOLE (gwa-kuh-MOH-lee)
Serves 6

Mexicans enjoy a very special sort of salad. They serve smooth green Guacamole made from avocado. Avocados are sometimes called alligator pears because their green skin is so leathery and tough. Inside that tough skin is soft delicious pulp with a large hard seed in the center.

For this recipe, the avocado *must* be ripe. To test for ripeness, gently squeeze the avocado between the palms of your hands. The fruit should be soft enough to give slightly.

INGREDIENTS

1 large ripe avocado	¾ t. salt
1½ T. lemon juice	1½ T. mayonnaise
1 small onion	dash of garlic salt
1 small tomato	crackers

EQUIPMENT

paring knife	fork
mixing bowl	mixing spoon
measuring spoons	

HOW TO MAKE:

1. Cut the avocado in half. Remove the seed.
2. Peel the avocado (or you can scoop the pulp out of the hard skin with a spoon).
3. Put the avocado pulp into the mixing bowl and add the lemon juice.
4. Mash the avocado, mixing the lemon juice into it with the fork.
5. Peel the onion and mince it into very small pieces.
6. Dice the tomato, and add it with the salt, mayonnaise, and garlic salt to the mashed avocado.
7. Stir until smooth.
8. Add the pieces of minced onion and mix well.
9. Serve the Guacamole with crackers or tortilla chips or as a filling for sandwiches.

NOTE: You might save the avocado seed and plant it.

4

A basic food of Central and South America and the islands of the Caribbean, is the kidney bean. Because kidney beans are rich in protein, they're often combined with corn or rice to make a nourishing meatless meal. One bean combination is so popular in Haiti that it's called *Plat National*, or national dish.

Haitian cooking is quite spicy, but we've made the hot pepper sauce in this recipe optional. If you want to be cautious, sprinkle a little on one part of your serving of rice and beans after you get to the table.

BEFORE BEGINNING! Dried kidney beans need to be softened before they're cooked, so plan ahead. Soak one day; cook the next. You can also use canned beans which don't need soaking.

INGREDIENTS

1 cup dried kidney beans (or 1 10-oz. can, drained)	pinch of ground cloves
3 cups water	1 t. salt
4 strips bacon	½ t. pepper
2 medium onions	few drops hot pepper sauce (optional)
1 cup uncooked rice	

EQUIPMENT

measuring cups	paper towel
mixing bowl	paring knife
saucepan	mixing spoon
large frying pan	serving platter
fork	

HOW TO MAKE:

NOTE: If canned beans are used, begin the recipe at step 4.

1. In the mixing bowl, soak the beans in water overnight. (A quicker way is to pour boiling water over the beans to cover. Let them stand 2 hours.)
2. Two hours before you want to serve them, put the beans and the water in which they soaked into the saucepan and bring them to a boil over moderate heat. There should be enough water to cover the beans. Add more if it is needed.
3. Let the beans simmer, covered, for an hour or more until they are tender.
4. Put the 4 strips of bacon into the frying pan and cook over low heat until the bacon is crisp and brown. Turn off the heat and remove the bacon to the paper towel. Pat it dry. Then pour all but 3 tablespoons of bacon grease out of the frying pan (pour it into an empty bowl or container).
5. Peel and dice the onions. Then put them into the frying pan with the 3 tablespoons of bacon grease.
6. Sauté the onion in the bacon grease over low heat for two minutes or more until the onion has turned golden in color.
7. Add the beans and the water to the frying pan. Stir.
8. Crumble the bacon. Add the rice, cloves, salt, pepper, and bacon to the beans. If you're using hot pepper sauce, now is the time to add a few drops. Stir well.
9. Let the mixture simmer for 45 minutes over low heat until the rice is soft. The water should all be gone when the rice is ready to serve. If the mixture gets too dry before the rice is done, add a little more water.
10. Turn it out onto a platter and serve at once.
11. Put the hot pepper sauce on the table for those who may like a more highly spiced taste.

BARBADOS

BANANA PUDDING
Makes 8 to 12 pieces

Banana means "fruit of the wise men." An early Roman scholar told of wise men in India who sat for days under banana plants eating the delicious fruit.

Today bananas are eaten all over the world. They grow best in hot and rainy areas like this island in the West Indies.

Be wise when buying bananas. Buy plump, firm, unbruised, bright yellow fruit. Bananas that are hard are not yet ripe. Leave them at room temperature for a day or two until they soften.

INGREDIENTS

4	bananas	1	cup milk
2	eggs		pinch of
6	slices of white bread		cinnamon
½	cup sugar	2	limes
½	t. vanilla	4	T. butter

EQUIPMENT

medium mixing bowl	paring knife
fork	small bowl
mixing spoon	small saucepan
measuring cups	8-in.-square baking
measuring spoons	pan

HOW TO MAKE:

1. Preheat the oven to 375°.
2. Peel the bananas. Put them in the mixing bowl and mash them with the fork.
3. Add the eggs, and beat them into the mashed bananas.
4. With your fingers crumble the slices of bread into crumbs.
5. Add the bread crumbs, sugar, vanilla, milk, and cinnamon to the banana mixture.
6. Cut the limes in half. Squeeze the juice into the small bowl.
7. Add the juice to the banana mixture. Stir all the ingredients well with the mixing spoon.
8. Melt the butter in the saucepan over low heat. Be careful not to let it burn. Add the melted butter to the mixture.
9. Beat the mixture 75 strokes.
10. Pour the mixture into the pan. Bake it at 375° for 1 hour. Remove the pudding from the oven and let it cool for 1 hour.
11. Cut it into squares.

VENEZUELA

BREAKFAST COCOA
Serves 2

Buenas días. It's morning in Venezuela. And the Venezuelans, like many other South Americans, enjoy starting the day with a cup of sweet hot cocoa.

Cocoa and chocolate come from the beans of the cacao tree, a tree native to Central and South America. Groves of these trees grow in countries where there are heavy rains and hot sun. So in South America, Central America, and Mexico, cocoa has been a favorite drink for hundreds of years.

INGREDIENTS

¼ cup water
3 T. cocoa
2 T. sugar

2 cups milk
1 t. vanilla

EQUIPMENT

measuring cup
medium saucepan
measuring spoons

mixing spoon
2 cups

HOW TO MAKE:

1. Bring the ¼ cup of water to a boil in the saucepan.
2. Stir in the cocoa and sugar until they are blended. Turn the heat very low.
3. Slowly pour the milk into the saucepan with the cocoa mixture. Stirring steadily to keep it from burning, cook it over low heat for about 2 minutes. Do not let it boil or skin will form on the top.
4. When the cocoa is hot, remove from the stove and stir in the vanilla.
5. Carefully pour the cocoa into the cups. Serve hot.

In Peru you can share an ear of corn on the cob, and still have plenty to eat yourself. Ears of corn—called *Choclos*—grow very large in Peru. At city street stands, *Choclos* are cooked over charcoal and sold piping hot. In homes, *Choclos* are steamed. Then they're broken into several pieces and eaten with the fingers.

The corn you use will probably not be as large as *Choclos*. But you can still share it. Break large ears in half. Steam them. Then spread the pieces with butter blends.

INGREDIENTS

4 ears of corn	salt
butter	cold water

EQUIPMENT

large saucepan and lid	kitchen tongs or long fork
	plate

HOW TO MAKE:

1. Remove the husks and silk from the corn. Rinse the corn.
2. Pour 1 inch of water into the saucepan.
3. Cover and bring the water to a boil over medium heat.
4. When the water is boiling, lift the lid and gently drop the corn into the water. Use the kitchen tongs or long fork.
5. When the water again starts to boil, cover the pot and cook the corn for 4 minutes.
6. Turn off the heat. Using the tongs or fork, carefully lift out the ears of corn and put them on the plate.
7. Let the corn cool for a few minutes. If your ears of corn are large, break them in half as the Peruvians do. Serve your *Choclos* with butter and salt. For a delicious change, try one of these Butter Blends.

Butter Blends
INGREDIENTS

¼ cup soft butter	¼ t. garlic salt
and	1 t. chopped parsley
2 t. grated lemon rind	**or**
or	⅛ cup tomato juice
½ t. salt	

EQUIPMENT

small bowl	mixing spoon
paring knife	pretty dish

HOW TO MAKE:

Lemon Butter. Blend the grated lemon rind and butter together in the small bowl. Serve in the pretty dish.

Herb Butter. Blend the soft butter with the salt, garlic salt, and chopped parsley.

Tomato Butter. Put the butter in the bowl and gradually add the tomato juice, stirring with the mixing spoon and blending well.

From
PARAGUAY
CORNBREAD
Makes 6 to 8 pieces 🖐🖐

When a Paraguayan family goes to an *asado* (a barbecue or picnic), crusty cornbread and beans are an important part of the meal. Both are popular foods in Paraguay, as they are in other South American countries. For special occasions, the cornbread is spiced with onions and cheese. This cornbread is called *Sopa Paraguaya.*

Since so many people like cornbread, there are many recipes for it. Here's a simple one, and one for *Sopa Paraguaya* a bit more complicated. Make one of them for your next *asado.*

INGREDIENTS

1	cup yellow cornmeal	1	t. salt
1	cup flour	1	egg
¼	cup sugar	1	cup milk
1	T. baking powder	1¼	cup butter
		1	or 2 t. butter

For *Sopa Paraguaya*

1	or 2 t. butter	4	ozs. (¼ lb.) Monterey Jack or Muenster cheese
1	small onion		

EQUIPMENT

measuring cups   fork
measuring spoons   small saucepan
large mixing bowl   8-in.-square baking
mixing spoon   pan
small bowl

For *Sopa Paraguaya*

paring knife   grater
small saucepan   piece of waxed paper

HOW TO MAKE:

1. Preheat the oven to 425°.
2. Put the cornmeal, flour, sugar, baking powder, and salt into the large bowl and stir well with the mixing spoon.
3. Break the egg into the small bowl and beat it lightly with the fork.
4. Make a hollow in the center of the dry ingredients and pour the beaten egg into it.
5. Add the milk and beat the mixture for a minute with the spoon.
6. Melt the butter in the small saucepan over low heat.
7. Fold the butter into the mixture.
8. Grease the baking pan with 1 or 2 teaspoons of butter. Pour in the cornbread batter.
9. Bake for 25 minutes. The top should be lightly browned. Test with a toothpick for doneness. (See page xiii.)
10. Cool for a few minutes. Cut into squares.
11. Serve while still warm. Any leftovers will be good cold the next day.

To Make *Sopa Paraguaya*

1. Peel the onion and mince it into small pieces.
2. Sauté the minced onion in 1 or 2 teaspoons of butter for about 2 minutes until it is light gold in color.
3. Grate the Monterey Jack (or Muenster) cheese with the coarse edge of the grater onto the piece of waxed paper.
4. Follow steps 1-6 in the directions for cornbread.
5. Fold the melted butter, onions, and grated cheese into the cornbread mixture.
6. Follow steps 8-10 above.

From

BRAZIL

GUAVA TOAST

Serves 2 ✋

Guava is a red or yellow fruit just about the size of your fist. Brazilians eat fresh guava slices as an early-morning snack or as a dessert with cream cheese.

Sometimes guava is made into jelly and served on toast. People say that guava tastes like strawberries. Try some and see for yourself.

INGREDIENTS

2	slices white bread	butter guava jelly

EQUIPMENT

knife   cookie sheet

HOW TO MAKE:

1. Preheat the oven to 375°.
2. Spread the butter on the bread.
3. Top it with the jelly.
4. Put the slices on a cookie sheet.
5. Bake them for 15 minutes. The bread will be lightly toasted.
6. Serve and eat the Guava Toast while it is hot.

From
MOROCCO
SUMMER SALADS
Serves 6 ♨♨

A Moroccan feast is a mixture of sweet, spicy, and tart foods. A main dish might be chicken smothered in lemons and olives or lamb baked with honey; a peppery fish might next be served; and for dessert, a honey-and-nut pastry. Glasses of mint tea are sipped throughout the meal. And between courses, there are cooling salads to eat, like the ones given here.

Salads like these may be a new idea to you. They're tart but tasty. When you've tried them, adjust the seasonings to suit your own taste.

Tangy Olives
INGREDIENTS

1   8-oz. can black olives
3   lemons

pinch of cayenne pepper
pinch of cumin (optional)

EQUIPMENT

paring knife   mixing bowl

HOW TO MAKE:

1. Drain the olives.
2. Peel the lemons and cut them into pieces about the size of the olives.
3. Combine the lemons with the olives in the mixing bowl.
4. Add the spices to the olives and lemon and toss gently to mix just before serving.

Chilled Oranges
INGREDIENTS

3   oranges
1   T. sugar

1   t. cinnamon

EQUIPMENT

paring knife   small bowl
measuring spoons   spoon

HOW TO MAKE:

1. Peel the oranges with your hands. Cut them into thick slices.
2. Mix the cinnamon and sugar in a small bowl.
3. Sprinkle the oranges with the cinnamon-sugar mix.
4. Toss them with a spoon. Chill them in the refrigerator for at least 10 minutes before serving.

Mixed Dice
INGREDIENTS

3   apples
2   green peppers
3   tomatoes
2   cucumbers

3   T. olive oil
1   T. lemon juice
    dash of salt and pepper

EQUIPMENT

paring knife   measuring spoons
mixing bowl   mixing spoon

HOW TO MAKE:

1. Cut out the seeds and hard core from the apples. Dice the apples.
2. Cut the green peppers in half and remove the seeds.
3. Dice the tomatoes, green pepper, and cucumber.
4. Place all the diced pieces in the mixing bowl. Add the olive oil and lemon juice.
5. Toss the salad until mixed. Season it with salt and pepper.
6. Serve the salad right away.

From
GHANA

FUFU—Mashed Vegetable
Serves 6

Mealtime in Ghana. An iron pot full of yams hangs over an open fire. Yams are an important energy food for Ghanians. In this recipe the yams are boiled, mashed, and rolled into balls called *Fufu*. In Ghana *Fufu* is often served with soup. The balls are placed in the soup bowl or dipped into the soup and eaten with the hands. You can serve your *Fufu* with soup or arranged on a plate as a vegetable.

NOTE: West African yams are pale yellow and floury. This recipe, however, has been adapted for yams or sweet potatoes found in the United States.

INGREDIENTS

1½ lbs. yams (about 3 yams) water	½ t. salt ⅛ t. pepper

EQUIPMENT

vegetable peeler	medium mixing bowl
paring knife	fork or masher
saucepan and cover	mixing spoon
small bowl	serving dish

HOW TO MAKE:

1. Wash and peel the yams. Cut them into half-inch slices.
2. Put the slices in the saucepan. Add enough hot water to cover them.
3. Place the saucepan on the stove. Bring the water and yams to a boil.
4. Cover the saucepan and reduce the heat a little.
5. Boil the yams gently until they are soft (a fork should go through them easily). This will take about 25 minutes.
6. Remove the saucepan from the stove and drain off the water into a small bowl.
7. Let the yams cool for 15 minutes.
8. Put a few slices of yam into the mixing bowl and mash them with the fork or masher.
9. Add salt and pepper and continue to add slices of yam and to mash them, a few at a time, until all the slices are mashed.
10. Beat the mashed yam with the mixing spoon until it is soft and free from lumps.
11. Roll the mixture into small balls. (If mixture seems too dry to stick together in a ball, moisten it with 1 tablespoon or more of the cooking liquid.)
12. Serve the *Fufu* in a warm dish—as a vegetable or with your favorite soup.

13

NIGERIA

GROUNDNUT SOUP

Serves 6 ✋✋

In Nigeria when it's time for *chop*, it's time for food—that's what *chop* means. One food that grows easily in this tropical country is the groundnut, or peanut as we call it. Protein-rich groundnuts are eaten in many ways: raw, roasted, boiled, pressed into cooking oil, and ground into butter. They're put into spicy stews, as well as into simple soups like this one. If you like the taste of peanuts, you'll like this groundnut soup.

INGREDIENTS

1	large tomato
1	large potato
1	medium onion
2	cups water
1	beef bouillon cube
1	t. salt

1 cup shelled, unsalted, roasted peanuts (you can use ½ cup peanut butter, crunchy or smooth, instead)

½ cup milk

2 T. rice

EQUIPMENT

vegetable peeler
paring knife
large saucepan and
lid

measuring cups
measuring spoons
chopper
medium bowl
mixing spoon

HOW TO MAKE:

1. Peel the potato and the onion.
2. Dice the potato, tomato, and onion into very small pieces.
3. Place in the saucepan with the 2 cups of water, the bouillon cube, and the salt.
4. Boil the mixture gently with the lid on for 30 minutes.
5. Chop the peanuts with the chopper or cut them into very small pieces with the knife. Put the nuts in the bowl and combine them with the milk. (If you are using peanut butter, mix it with the milk until it is smooth.)
6. Add the peanut mixture and the rice to the potato, tomato, onion, and water.
7. Mix well with a spoon.
8. Lower the heat and cook at a simmer for 30 minutes or more.
9. Pour into soup bowls and serve.

In the 1500's, Portuguese explorers landing at the mouth of a river on the west coast of Africa spotted hundreds of small pink prawns. They called the river "Rio dos Camaroes" (river of prawns). The West African land of Cameroon takes its name from this river.

Today the river still teems with prawns. They appear on menus all over Cameroon. Prawns (river shrimp) from Cameroon aren't available in this country, but shrimp taste very much the same.

INGREDIENTS

1	t. butter	1	t. paprika
20	medium shrimp		pinch of pepper
½	cup fresh parsley	½	cup olive oil
1	t. salt	½	lemon

EQUIPMENT

8-in. baking dish   measuring spoons
paring knife   measuring cups
paper towel   mixing spoon
small bowl   serving platter

HOW TO MAKE:

1. Lightly butter the baking dish.
2. Clean and wash the shrimp. The shells of fresh shrimp are easily removed with your hands. (It's a little like shelling peanuts.) The black vein down the back of each shelled shrimp should also be removed. Use the paring knife. Pat the shrimp dry with the paper towel.
3. Arrange the shrimp side by side in the baking dish.
4. Wash the parsley. Put a few sprigs aside to decorate the serving platter. With the paring knife, chop the rest of the parsley into very small pieces.
5. In the small bowl, mix the salt, paprika, parsley, and pepper.
6. Add the olive oil to these ingredients and stir with the mixing spoon.
7. Spread the olive-oil mixture over the shrimp.
8. Put the shrimp in the refrigerator to marinate for 1 to 2 hours.
9. Remove the shrimp from the refrigerator and let them stand for 15 minutes.
10. Adjust the broiler rack to its middle level and preheat the broiler.
11. Cut the lemon into wedges or slices.
12. Broil the shrimp in the baking dish for 3 minutes. Turn them over. Broil them for 3 more minutes. The shrimp are done when they are pink.
13. Serve on the platter with the lemon and the pieces of parsley.

NOTE: Ask a grown-up to help you with the broiling. If frozen shrimp are used, let them thaw for 30 minutes. Frozen shrimp are usually small, so you will need about 30 of them to make this recipe.

ZAIRE

SIMPLE AFRICAN STEW
Serves 4 to 6

This meal-in-a-pot is from Zaire, but stews very much like it are popular in most African countries. There are as many variations to a stew as there are cooks who make it. The suggestions at the end of this recipe are ingredients that might be found in a stew pot in Zaire. Make the stew the first time the way it is in the recipe; then add foods to suit your own taste. Lovers of spicier stew should add ½ to 1 teaspoon of cayenne pepper. Be careful when using cayenne pepper though. Too much will burn your tongue!

INGREDIENTS

2	onions	1	t. salt
¼	cup vegetable oil or peanut oil	½	t. pepper
1	chicken (2½ to 3 lbs.) cut into serving pieces	1	cup water
		2	cups tomato juice
1	tomato		cayenne pepper (optional)

EQUIPMENT

paring knife
measuring cups
stewing pot (or Dutch oven) with lid
paper towels

spatula or large spoon
measuring spoons
plate

HOW TO MAKE:

1. Peel and chop the onions.
2. Dry the chicken with the paper towels. (If the chicken is wet, it will not brown properly.)
3. Heat the oil in the pot over medium heat for a minute.
4. Place the chicken and the onions in the pot and brown on all sides, turning the chicken with the spatula, large spoon, or tongs.
5. Remove the chicken and onions to a plate. Drain the excess oil from the pot. Put 2 tablespoons of the oil back in the pot with the chicken and the onions.
6. Cut the tomato into wedges.
7. Add the tomato, salt, pepper, water, and tomato juice to the pot.
8. Cover the stew and lower the heat. Let it simmer for about 45 minutes.
9. Remove the pieces of chicken to a plate. Cover them to keep them warm.
10. Blend 3 tablespoons of flour and 3 tablespoons of hot water in a small bowl. Pour the flour-and-water mixture into the gravy in the stew pot. Stir over medium heat until the mixture slightly thickens.
11. Pour the gravy from the stew pot over the chicken.

VARIATIONS: Add some or all of these extra ingredients to your stew: 1 green pepper, seeded and diced; 1 or 2 plantains, peeled and sliced into 2-in. pieces; 2 or 3 potatoes (sweet or white), peeled and sliced; ½ cup unsalted peanuts.

Ugandans don't eat dessert, but they like to snack on sweet ripe fruit and pieces of sugarcane. Uganda's hot wet climate is ideal for growing fruit, so there are many kinds to choose from. Favorite Ugandan fruits that are also available in this country are yellow bananas, peeled and eaten raw, cubes of fresh pineapple, orange sections, and slices of pawpaw (sometimes pawpaw is called papaya).

INGREDIENTS

2	oranges	3	bananas
1	papaya (or a small canteloupe or honeydew melon)	1	or 2 limes

EQUIPMENT

paring knife   platter, plate, or
                              large shallow dish

HOW TO MAKE:

1. With your fingers, peel the oranges. Separate the fruit into sections. Put them to one side.
2. Cut the papaya (or melon) in half. Scoop out the seeds. Then cut each half into slices. They should be about 1 inch thick at their thickest part. When you have cut all the slices, turn them on their sides, one at a time. Cut the rind from each piece and set the slices aside.
3. Just before serving, peel the bananas. (If you let bananas stand too long after they're peeled, they will turn brown.)
4. Cut the bananas in half lengthwise, from top to bottom.
5. Arrange the banana slices so that they radiate from the center of the platter like the spokes of a wheel.
6. Put the orange slices and the papaya (or melon) slices between the banana slices.
7. Cut one of the limes in half the long way (from end to end). Cut the halves in half. Then cut those pieces in half again. This will give you 8 pieces of lime.
8. Arrange the pieces of lime on the platter with the other fruit.
9. If you want to put the fruit platter on a buffet table, cut the other lime in half and squeeze the juice from half of it over the bananas. Lime juice (or lemon juice) keeps bananas from turning brown.

VARIATIONS: Use any other fruits in season. Apples, strawberries, pineapple, peaches, pears, watermelon—the list is endless. Use your own imagination. For an extra treat, ice cream or fresh cream can be served over all.

From
ICELAND
BAKED ATLANTIC FISH
Serves 6 ✸✸

Fish is king in Iceland, where such salt-water fish as cod, haddock, and herring abound. Icelanders live in the coastal areas of their island, and many of them earn their living by fishing. Fish are the country's number one resource. Naturally, Icelanders eat fish often.

INGREDIENTS

½ T. butter
6 fish fillets (sole, haddock, cod, or halibut)
1 lemon
¼ t. salt
¼ t. pepper
¼ t. paprika

6 ozs. ungrated Swiss cheese (1½ cups grated)
½ T. dry mustard
1 cup heavy cream
½ cup bread crumbs

EQUIPMENT

shallow baking dish
measuring spoons
paring knife
grater

measuring cups
small bowl
mixing spoon

HOW TO MAKE:

1. Preheat oven to 350°.
2. Grease the baking dish with the butter.
3. If fresh fillets are used, place them in the dish. If frozen fillets are used, leave them at room temperature until they're thawed. Then place them in the dish.
4. Cut the lemon in half.
5. Sprinkle one side of the fillets with half the salt, pepper, and paprika. Squeeze the juice from one half of the lemon on the fillets.
6. Turn the fillets over. Repeat step 5 on this side of the fillets.
7. Grate the Swiss cheese. Sprinkle it evenly over the fish.
8. Put the dry mustard into the small mixing bowl. Mix in the cream. Pour the mixture over the fish.
9. Sprinkle the bread crumbs over the fish.
10. Bake in the oven at 350° for 35 minutes.

19

From
PORTUGAL

RABANADAS (rah-bah-NAH-dahs)—
Sweet Toast
Serves 4   ♥♥

The Portuguese cook, eat, and talk about their food with pleasure, especially at holiday times. Then there's no skimping on delicious sweets. Many are sprinkled with cinnamon and sugar like these *Rabanadas*, a Christmastime specialty. In Portugal, *Rabanadas* is served with boiled fish and potatoes and with a rich rice pudding on Christmas Eve.

You'll find this recipe has a lot in common with French toast, which is often eaten in this country. Don't wait for Christmas Eve—have *Rabanadas* for your next meal.

INGREDIENTS

¾ cup milk
2   T. sugar
4   slices white bread

2   eggs
2   T. butter
1   t. cinnamon

EQUIPMENT

measuring cups
saucepan

small bowl
fork

measuring spoons
mixing spoon
shallow baking pan

large frying pan
wide spatula
plate

HOW TO MAKE:

1. Measure the ¾ cup of milk into the saucepan and cook it over low heat until it is hot but not boiling.
2. Add 1 tablespoon of the sugar. Stir. Remove the mixture from heat and pour it into the baking pan.
3. Put the 4 slices of bread into the milk and sugar in the baking pan to soak up the mixture.
4. Crack the eggs into the small bowl and beat them with the fork.
5. Melt the butter in the frying pan over low heat.
6. While the butter is melting, remove the slices of bread (one at a time) from the milk. Dip each slice into the beaten egg and turn, so that both sides of the bread are coated.
7. Place the pieces of bread in the frying pan. The edges can touch, but they should not overlap. If all 4 slices of bread do not fit in the frying pan, cook 2 pieces at a time.
8. Sauté the pieces until they are golden brown on their underside. Turn the pieces over with the spatula. Sauté the other sides until they too are golden.
9. With the spatula, remove them to a plate.
10. Mix the remaining 1 T. of sugar with the cinnamon. Sprinkle the mixture over the *Rabanadas*. Serve warm.

From

ENGLAND

TEA AND SUGAR CRISPS
Tea for 2
Makes 15 to 20 cookies 🐾🐾

Teatime for the English—after-school snacktime for you. Do as the English do and sip tea along with Sugar Crisps.

Anyone can make what the English call a "proper cup of tea," if they follow these simple directions and remember to take the teapot to the kettle—not the kettle to the teapot. Read the recipe and see what we mean.

If you positively can't get loose tea, then use teabags. The English consider teabags a Yankee invention and the ruin of a good cup of tea, but even so they admit teabags are convenient.

Tea
INGREDIENTS

2½ cups water	½ cup milk or
3 t. tea (or 3 teabags)	2 slices lemon sugar

EQUIPMENT

teakettle
measuring cup
teapot

measuring spoon
two cups

HOW TO MAKE:

1. Put the water in the teakettle and set it on the stove to heat.
2. When the water is hot, pour about half a cup of it from the kettle into the teapot. This will warm the teapot.
3. When the water in the kettle starts to boil, pour out all the hot water in the teapot and put the tea (or teabags) into the teapot.
4. Bring the teapot to the stove. Remove the kettle from the heat, and while the water is still bubbling, carefully pour it into the teapot.
5. Put the lid on the teapot and let the mixture "steep" (stand and brew) for 3 to 5 minutes.
6. Pour a little cold milk into the two cups. Pour in the tea. (You may want to use a tea strainer to keep the tea leaves from falling in.) Serve with sugar.

NOTE: Some people prefer lemon in their tea. In that case leave out the milk and add a slice of lemon to each cup.

Sugar Crisps
INGREDIENTS

¼ cup (½ stick) soft butter	½ cup flour few drops vanilla
¼ cup sugar	1 or 2 t. milk

EQUIPMENT

measuring cups
medium mixing bowl
mixing spoon

measuring spoon
large cookie sheet or
two small ones

sifter
piece of waxed paper

spatula
wire rack

HOW TO MAKE:

1. Preheat the oven to 350°.
2. Measure the butter and sugar into the mixing bowl, and stir them together with the spoon until they are well blended.
3. Sift the ½ cup of flour onto the waxed paper. Add it to the butter-and-sugar mixture, a little at a time. Beat well after each addition.
4. Add the vanilla and 1 teaspoon of milk to the mixture.
5. Stir until the mixture does not stick to the sides of the bowl. If it seems too dry and floury, add one more teaspoon of milk.
6. With your hands, form the dough into a smooth ball.
7. Pinch off about 1 teaspoon of dough. Roll it between your palms into a small ball.
8. Place the ball on an ungreased cookie sheet. Flatten it with your palm or the bottom of a glass.
9. Continue until all the dough is used up. Place the balls at least 1 inch apart.
10. Put them in the center of the oven and let them bake for 10 minutes. Check to see if the crisps are golden brown. If not, bake them a few more minutes. Keep watching them to make sure they don't burn.
11. Remove the crisps from the oven and let them cool for 5 minutes. Lift cookies off with spatula and place them on a wire rack to finish cooling.

IRELAND

BROONIE—Irish Gingerbread

Makes 6 pieces ꙮꙮꙮ

The Irish are famous for home-baked potato bread and soda bread. Both are unusual and flavorful. Less well known but just as good is Broonie, an Irish bread that's almost a cake. Broonie is chewy and dark in color. It is full of oats —a grain grown in this cool, wet land. Broonie, which is a little sweet, blends perfectly with hot tea or cold milk.

INGREDIENTS

1	or 2 t. butter	1	t. ground ginger
2	cups flour	¾	t. salt
1½	t. baking soda	½	cup soft butter
1	t. cinnamon	½	cup sugar
1	egg	½	cup quick-cooking oatmeal
2	egg yolks		
1	cup molasses	1	cup hot water

EQUIPMENT

8-in.-square baking pan	sifter
measuring cups	piece of waxed paper
measuring spoons	mixing bowl
	mixing spoon

HOW TO MAKE:

1. Preheat the oven to 350°.
2. Grease the bottom of the baking pan with 1 or 2 teaspoons of butter.
3. Measure the flour, baking soda, cinnamon, ginger, and salt and sift them together onto the piece of waxed paper.
4. In the mixing bowl, combine the butter with the sugar by stirring them with the mixing spoon until they are well blended.
5. Add the egg and egg yolks. (If you don't know how to separate the egg yolks from the whites, see the directions for Eggs on page vii.)
6. With the mixing spoon, beat the mixture until it is fluffy.
7. Stir in the molasses.
8. Add the sifted dry ingredients, the oatmeal, and the hot water one fourth at a time to the egg-and-molasses mixture, stirring after each addition.
9. Pour the mixture into the greased pan.
10. Bake the Broonie 50 to 55 minutes. Test with a toothpick for doneness. (See page xiii.)
11. Cut into squares and serve warm.

GINGER

Long loaves of bread as only the French can make it, crusty on the outside and soft on the inside, are the beginnings of this melt-in-your-mouth sandwich. A *croque* is a sandwich dipped in an egg mixture and fried. The French call the combination of bread, ham, and cheese in this recipe *Croque Monsieur.* Topped with a fried egg, it's a *Croque Madame.*

Try this recipe. Then invent a *croque* of your own. Note: *Croques* can be made with French bread or regular white bread. *Bon appetit!*

INGREDIENTS

4	slices cooked ham	4	slices Swiss cheese
8	slices bread	¼	cup milk
2	eggs	2	T. butter

EQUIPMENT

paring knife
medium bowl
fork or egg beater

large frying pan
wide spatula

HOW TO MAKE:

1. Trim the ham and the cheese with the paring knife to fit the bread.
2. Make a sandwich by placing 1 slice of ham and 1 slice of cheese between 2 slices of bread. Make 3 more sandwiches the same way.
3. Crack the eggs into the mixing bowl, add the milk, and beat them together well.
4. Melt the butter in the frying pan over low heat. Be careful the butter doesn't burn.
5. While the butter is melting, dip each side of each sandwich into the egg-and-milk mixture.
6. When the butter is hot and bubbling, place the sandwiches side by side in the frying pan. Sauté them over medium heat for about 3 minutes until they're golden brown on the bottom. To see if they are brown enough, lift a corner of the sandwich with the spatula and peek at the underside. When they are done, turn them with the spatula and cook the other side.
7. Sauté the other side for 3 minutes or until it browns and the cheese melts.
8. Serve at once.

They look a little like toadstools, but they're not. They taste a little like deviled eggs, but they're not. They're Padstools from Belgium. Padstools are easy to make, fun to serve, and good to eat.

Belgian cooks make sure that food looks and tastes very fresh. They use crisp lettuce and parsley, and juicy ripe tomatoes right from the garden or store. That is what makes Padstools such a refreshing appetizer or luncheon dish.

INGREDIENTS

4	eggs	2	T. mayonnaise
2	T. parsley	4	lettuce leaves
½	cup cooked shrimp (fresh, canned, or frozen)	2	small red tomatoes

EQUIPMENT

paring knife
small mixing bowl
fork
measuring cup

measuring spoon
mixing spoon
paper towel

HOW TO MAKE:

1. Hard-cook the eggs. (If you don't know how to do this, see the directions under Eggs on page vii.)

2. Peel off the shells.
3. Cut off a slice from the blunt end of each egg and put it aside.
4. Remove the egg yolks. Be careful to leave the egg whites whole.
5. Cut off a slice from the other end of each egg, so that the egg will stand up straight.
6. In the mixing bowl, mash the egg yolks with the fork.
7. Chop the parsley and shrimp into very small pieces and mix them with the egg yolks.
8. Add the mayonnaise to the shrimp and egg-yolk mixture and stir it to make a thick paste.

9. Stuff each egg white with one fourth of the mixture.
10. Wash the lettuce leaves and pat them dry on the paper towel. Place each egg on a lettuce leaf.
11. Cut the tomatoes in half crosswise.
12. Scoop out the centers from the tomato halves and place a tomato cup upside down on the top of each egg.
13. Chop the leftover bits of egg white and decorate the tomato cups with them.

NOTE: Keep the tomato insides. Cut them into small pieces and place them on the lettuce around the finished Padstools.

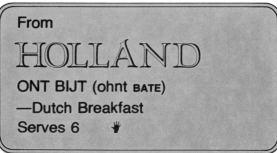

From
HOLLAND

ONT BIJT (ohnt BATE)
—Dutch Breakfast
Serves 6 ✋

Ont Bijt means breakfast in Dutch. And the Dutch don't skimp on the day's first meal. It is filled with the rich dairy foods produced in Holland—especially cheeses of all kinds. They start with slices of cheese on zweiback toast or Holland rusks. Then they eat slices of meat on fresh bread. Do as the Dutch do: choose two or three from Column A and two from Column B.

NOTE: The amounts given in the list of ingredients are approximate. *Ont Bijt* is a great way to stretch leftover roasts or a few pieces of sandwich meat. For example, if there isn't enough ham to go around, add some extra salami to the meat platter. First come, first served.

INGREDIENTS

Column A — Cheeses		Column B — Meats	
¼	lb. Edam	4	slices ham
1	lb. Gouda	4	slices roast beef
¼	Muenster	4	slices salami
¼	Swiss	4	slices bologna
¼	Leiden	4	slices liverwurst
	your favorite breads and crackers		butter jelly or jam

EQUIPMENT

knife   platter
cutting board

HOW TO MAKE:

1. Slice the cheeses and meats.
2. Arrange them on the platter with the breads and crackers.
3. Put your choice of cheese or meat on a slice of bread and make a sandwich with no top (it's called an open-face sandwich).

Cakes and pastries aren't eaten just for dessert in Germany. They are so well liked that they're often served by themselves. Special shops sell only sweets and drinks. Many Germans stop in for a late morning or afternoon snack —or both! A favorite order is a piece of torte (a word used for all sorts of cakes). Some tortes are filled or topped with whipped cream. The Chocolate Torte in this recipe can be topped with whipped cream or with ice cream or eaten plain.

INGREDIENTS

½ cup water
3 oz. sweet cooking
   chocolate
2 eggs
1½ cups sugar
½ cup soft butter
   pinch of salt

1 t. vanilla
¾ cup buttermilk
1 t. baking soda
1½ cups flour
1 or 2 t. butter

For topping

½ pint heavy cream
  (whipping cream)

1 T. sugar
½ t. vanilla

EQUIPMENT

measuring cups
heavy-bottomed
  saucepan
mixing spoon
large mixing bowl
egg beater
measuring spoons

medium bowl
sifter
waxed paper
8-in.-square baking
  pan
chilled mixing bowl
knife

HOW TO MAKE:

1. Preheat the oven to 375°.
2. Bring the water to a boil in the saucepan. Add the chocolate and stir it with the mixing spoon over medium heat until the chocolate melts. Watch it carefully so it doesn't burn.
3. Remove from the heat and let cool.
4. In the large bowl, beat the eggs until they are thick and lemon-colored. Beat in the sugar a little at a time.
5. When the eggs and sugar are well combined, beat in the butter and salt.
6. Add the melted chocolate and stir it well.
7. Add the vanilla and stir again.
8. In the medium bowl, combine the buttermilk and baking soda.
9. Sift the flour onto waxed paper.
10. Add the buttermilk and flour a third at a time to the chocolate mixture. Beat after each addition.
11. Grease the baking pan with the butter.
12. Pour the batter into the pan. Spread it evenly.
13. Bake it for 35 minutes. Test the cake with a toothpick for doneness. (See page xiii.)
14. Let the cake cool in the pan.
15. Just before you serve the cake, make the whipped cream. Pour the chilled heavy cream into the chilled bowl. (Whipping cream is easier if everything is cold.)
16. Beat the cream with the egg beater until it thickens enough to form soft peaks. (Do not beat it longer. If you beat it too long whipped cream will turn to butter.) Gently fold in the sugar and vanilla. Cut the cake into squares and top each square with whipped cream.

From

SWEDEN

MEAT BALLS
Serves 4 ♣♣♣

The original meaning of the word *smorgasbord* was sandwich board. Long ago the Vikings used a flat piece of bread as a plate and piled their other foods on top of it. Today a smorgasbord is a buffet.

The table is set with many different kinds of hot and cold foods. Swedes have a special order for arranging them: dishes of cold fish first; then cold meat; next, small hot dishes (such as these Meat Balls); and finally dessert. The foods you select are piled on a plate, but bread is still a must on the table.

You don't need to have a smorgasbord to enjoy these Meat Balls. They make a delightful dish for lunch, dinner, or Sunday brunch.

INGREDIENTS

¾ cup bread crumbs	2 t. salt
1 cup cream	½ t. ground allspice
1 onion	2 T. butter
1 egg	2 T. flour
1½ lbs. ground beef	1½ cups milk

EQUIPMENT

measuring cups	mixing spoon
medium mixing bowl	measuring spoons
paring knife	plate
small bowl	frying pan and cover
fork	serving platter

HOW TO MAKE:

1. Measure the bread crumbs and ½ cup of the cream into the mixing bowl. Let it sit for 5 minutes.
2. With the paring knife, peel the onion and chop it up into small pieces.
3. Break the egg into the small bowl and beat it with the fork.
4. Add the meat and the cut-up onion to the bread crumbs and cream. Mix well.
5. Stir in the egg, the salt, and the allspice.
6. Pick up a small amount of the mixture—about as big as a plum—with your hand. Roll it between your palms. Shape it into a ball. Place each ball when you have made it on the plate. Continue until all the meat is rolled into balls.
7. Melt the butter in the frying pan, over low heat.
8. Place a few meat balls in the pan. Roll them from side to side with the spoon till they are browned on all sides. Remove them to a plate. Continue until all the balls are browned. Turn off the heat.
9. Add the flour to the frying pan. Stir it with the fat and meat juice until it is all mixed together. Scrape up the meat that has stuck to the bottom of the pan with the mixing spoon.
10. Add the second ½ cup of cream and the milk to the mixture in the pan. Stir it until it makes a smooth sauce.
11. Return the meat balls to the frying pan with the sauce. Cover the pan with a lid.
12. Simmer it over a very low flame for 25 minutes.
13. Arrange the meat balls on the serving platter and pour the gravy over them.

27

From

FINLAND

BERRY SHAKE
Serves 2 ✋

Red lingonberries, yellow cloudberries, blueberries, deep red raspberries— colorful and delicate berries of all kinds are grown and eaten in Finland. Fresh berries are mixed into desserts or drinks like this Berry Shake. Use strawberries for your first shake. Then create a berry shake of your own.

INGREDIENTS

10 fresh strawberries
or
6 T. frozen sliced strawberries in syrup (thawed)

2 cups cold milk
1½ T. sugar or honey

EQUIPMENT

paring knife
measuring cups
small bowl

measuring spoons
egg beater
2 glasses

HOW TO MAKE:

1. Wash the strawberries (if fresh) and cut out the stems.
2. Cut the strawberries into small pieces. (If you're using frozen strawberries, drain the syrup into a small bowl or cup and save it for step 4.)
3. Pour the milk into the mixing bowl. Add the strawberries.
4. If you're using fresh strawberries, add the sugar or honey. If you're using frozen strawberries, add 3 tablespoons of the strawberry syrup instead of sugar.
5. Beat with the egg beater for one minute.
6. Pour the drink into the glasses.

From

POLAND

ZUPA NIC (zoo-pah NITTS)—Nothing Soup

Serves 4 to 6 ♟ ♟

Something scrumptious . . . from nothing. That's why this soup is called *nic* (nothing) in Polish. To make it you need nothing special—the ingredients are milk, eggs, sugar, and vanilla—but the results are quite unusual.

Poles might start a meal with this soup. It can also be served as a light snack or even as a dessert. Any way you have it, you'll find it's "nothing" but delicious.

INGREDIENTS

2	eggs	¼	cup milk
¼	cup sugar		dash of
1	T. sugar		cinnamon
1	qt. milk	1	T. vanilla

EQUIPMENT

2 mixing bowls   large saucepan
egg beater   mixing spoon
measuring cups   soup bowls or cups
measuring spoons

HOW TO MAKE:

1. Separate the eggs. (If you don't know how, see under Eggs on page vii.)
2. Beat the yolks with the egg beater, gradually adding the sugar until the mixture is thick and lemon-colored (about 2 minutes).
3. Wash and dry the egg beater and then beat the egg whites until they will stand in peaks by themselves and look dry and glossy. Beat in the tablespoon of sugar.
4. Pour the milk into the saucepan. Heat the milk until bubbles appear around the edges. Then lower the heat until it is simmering gently.
5. With the mixing spoon, drop spoonfuls of the egg whites on top of the milk (you probably won't use up all the egg whites). Try to keep the spoonfuls separated. Let them cook for two minutes. Turn them over with the spoon and cook two minutes more. Do not let the milk boil over. If it comes near the top of the saucepan, lower the heat.
6. Gently remove the cooked egg whites from the milk and place them in the soup bowls or cups.
7. Remove the saucepan from the heat.
8. Add the ¼ cup of cold milk to the beaten egg yolks.
9. Slowly pour the yolks into the hot milk in the saucepan, stirring as you do so.
10. Stir in the cinnamon and vanilla.
11. Carefully pour the soup over the cooked egg whites in the soup bowls.

From

HUNGARY

LIPTOI CHEESE (LIP-toy-ee)

Serves 4 to 6

Hungarians often season their food with paprika, a powder made from sweet red peppers. Paprika as we know it in this country is generally mild in taste, but in Hungary it varies from mild to very strong.

Paprika adds flavor to this smooth cheese blend. Eat it spread on crackers or slices of pumpernickel bread. The caraway seeds, another Hungarian favorite cooking ingredient, are a crunchy must.

INGREDIENTS

1 8-oz. pkg. soft cream cheese	1 T. paprika
¼ c. soft butter	1 t. dry mustard
1 t. salt	1½ T. caraway seeds

EQUIPMENT

medium mixing bowl   measuring spoons
mixing spoon   small serving bowl

HOW TO MAKE:

1. Blend the cheese and butter in the mixing bowl.
2. Add the remaining ingredients.
3. Mix them well. Put the blended cheese into the small serving bowl.
4. Chill in the refrigerator for at least 30 minutes before serving.

31

From
ITALY
ANTIPASTO PLATTER
Serves 4 to 6 ✋

Early Romans sometimes wore lettuce and parsley wreaths on their heads. The greens kept them cool during long banquets. Today Italians use these same greens, but instead of wearing them, they eat them.

Arranged on a platter, finger foods garnished with lettuce and parsley make up this colorful Antipasto. In Italy Antipasto is eaten before the *pasta*—spaghetti, macaroni, or noodles. You could serve it for a party or with a meal as salad or appetizer, or even as the main course of a light lunch.

INGREDIENTS

6	slices salami	½	melon (not watermelon)
3	eggs		
2	tomatoes	3	slices ham
1	green pepper	6	or 8 lettuce leaves
3	slices hard cheese		fresh parsley
6	celery stalks		black and green olives
1	3-oz. pkg. soft cream cheese	2	T. vinegar
2	t. chives (dried or fresh)	4	T. olive oil
			pinch of salt and pepper

EQUIPMENT

toothpicks	table knife
paring knife	paper towel
spoon	platter
small bowl	empty jar and lid
measuring spoons	

HOW TO MAKE:

1. Hard-cook the eggs. (If you don't know how to do this, see the directions under Eggs on page vii.)
2. Roll each piece of salami (like a tube) and fasten it with a toothpick.
3. Peel the hard-cooked eggs and slice them in half lengthwise.
4. Slice the tomatoes in wedges. Remove the seeds from the center of the green pepper and slice the green pepper in long strips. Cut the cheese into chunks about 1 in. square.
5. Wash the celery and cut it into pieces about 3 in. long.
6. For the celery filling, mash the cream cheese with the spoon in the small bowl. Mix in the chives. (If you use fresh ones, cut them in small pieces first.)
7. With the knife, put about a tablespoon of the filling in each piece of celery.
8. Slice the melon into strips about 3 in. long and 1 in. wide. This will be easier to manage if you cut the melon into four pieces and cut off the rind before cutting it into strips.
9. Cut the ham slices in half. Wrap a piece of ham around each strip of melon and fasten it in place with a toothpick.
10. Wash the lettuce leaves in water and pat dry on the paper towel. Place lettuce leaves on a large platter. Arrange everything as attractively as you can. Decorate the platter with parsley and olives.
11. Make a dressing for the Antipasto by combining the vinegar, oil, salt, and pepper in the jar. Cover the jar and shake it well. (An old mustard jar or a jelly jar with a screw-on top works well for shaking dressing.)
12. Sprinkle the dressing over the Antipasto and serve.

This square pie is probably different from anything you've ever tasted — unless you're Greek. In many Greek homes and restaurants, spinach pie (called *spanakopita*) is made with a crust of paper-thin *filo* pastry. Our version is a no-crust spinach pie. After it's baked, cut it into squares and serve it either by itself as a first course, or as part of the main course. In either case, your guests will say, *"Efharisto,"* which means thank you in Greek.

INGREDIENTS

1	pkg. frozen chopped spinach (10 oz. size)	4	eggs
½	lb. feta cheese (or sharp cheddar cheese)	6	T. flour
		½	t. salt
		½	t. pepper
1	pt. (2 cups) cottage cheese	1	or 2 t. butter

EQUIPMENT

fork (or grater)
2 mixing bowls
mixing spoon
measuring spoons

9-in.-square baking pan
table knife
platter

HOW TO MAKE:

1. Take the spinach from the freezer and let it thaw unopened. (Thawing will take at least 1 hour.)
2. Preheat the oven to 350°.
3. Crumble the feta cheese with the fork (or grate the cheddar cheese).
4. Drain the thawed spinach.
5. In one of the mixing bowls, mix the feta (or cheddar) cheese with the thawed spinach and the cottage cheese.
6. In the other bowl, mix the eggs, flour, salt, and pepper.
7. Combine the two mixtures in one bowl and mix well.
8. Grease the baking pan with 1 or 2 teaspoons of butter.
9. Pour the mixture into the pan and spread it evenly.
10. Bake the pie for one hour. To test for doneness, stick the tip of the table knife into the center. If the knife comes out clean, the pie is done.
11. Remove it from the oven and let it cool a few minutes.
12. Cut it into squares. Place it on the platter. Serve it while it's hot.

RUSSIA

SIRNIKI (SEER-nih-kee)—Bite-Sized Pancakes

Makes 25 little pancakes

Eat family style. That means passing platters of food around the table. Diners take as much or little as they want.

In Russia where the custom started, meals were often long and filling. First, appetizers such as caviar, herring, or other fish were passed. Then came soup, meat, potatoes, and other vegetables. A dessert like *Sirniki* might end the meal.

Sirniki doesn't have to be served as dessert. It's a meal in the hand, good for breakfast, lunch, dinner, or snacktime. Serve it the Russian way—with sour cream. The pancakes should be small enough to pick up and eat in one bite.

INGREDIENTS

½ cup (4 oz.) soft cream cheese	1 cup cottage cheese
2 eggs	4 T. butter
1 T. sugar	½ cup (¼ pt.) sour cream
½ t. salt	
½ cup flour	

EQUIPMENT

2 large mixing bowls	waxed paper
measuring cups	egg beater
mixing spoon	frying pan
measuring spoons	spatula
sifter	covered dish

HOW TO MAKE:

1. In one of the mixing bowls, mash the cream cheese with the spoon until it's smooth.
2. Separate the eggs (see Eggs, page vii for directions.) Put the whites into the other mixing bowl, the yolks in the bowl with the cream cheese.
3. Mix the egg yolks, the sugar, and the salt with the cream cheese.
4. Sift the flour onto the waxed paper.
5. Stir the cottage cheese into the cream cheese mixture. Then add the flour.
6. Mix it well to make a smooth batter.
7. Beat the egg whites with the egg beater until they are stiff and will hold a peak by themselves.
8. Fold the beaten egg whites into the batter.
9. Heat 2 tablespoons of butter in the frying pan until it sizzles. Don't let the butter burn.
10. Drop the batter by heaping tablespoons into the frying pan to form pancakes. Brown on one side for about two minutes.
11. With the metal spatula, turn the pancakes. Brown them for two more minutes.
12. Remove them from the frying pan. Put them in the covered dish to keep warm while you make the rest of the pancakes.
13. Prepare the rest of the pancakes the same way as the first (steps 9, 10, and 11).
14. Continue until all the batter is used up.
15. Place some sour cream on each pancake. Eat them folded in half, one on top of another like a sandwich, or open-face.

Long ago, soldiers cooked their meals over an open fire. Chunks of meat were threaded on swords and roasted. This was *shish kebab*—sword meat.

Today a kebab is any food broiled or grilled on skewers or cooking sticks. Food lovers of many nations enjoy eating kebabs of meat, fish, vegetables, or a mixture of all three.

The Turkish recipe for kebabs, given here uses lamb and fresh vegetables. Kebabs are often served with rice. A recipe for rice appears on page 42.

You might also make a Turkish sandwich. Put the cooked kebabs in the hollow center of a loaf of pita.

NOTE: Pita bread is sold in many large supermarkets and food specialty stores. Sometimes it is called Middle Eastern flat bread or Sahara bread.

INGREDIENTS

1½ lbs. shoulder of lamb (without the bone)	¼ cup olive oil
	2 T. lemon juice
3 tomatoes	1 t. salt
1 large green pepper	¼ t. pepper

EQUIPMENT

cutting knife
paring knife
chopping board
measuring cups

measuring spoons
medium mixing bowl
4 skewers, 12 in.
long

HOW TO MAKE:

1. Cut the lamb into 1-in. cubes (or ask your butcher to do it for you). (The precut lamb sold in markets and labeled lamb stew needs to be cooked for a long time to be tender. It does not usually make good kebabs.)
2. Cut the tomatoes into wedges.
3. Remove the seeds in the center of the green pepper and cut it into 1-in. squares.
4. Mix the oil, lemon juice, salt, and pepper in the mixing bowl.
5. Add the meat and the cut vegetables.
6. Let the meat and vegetables marinate for two hours or longer.
7. Preheat the broiler.
8. Remove the meat and vegetables from the bowl. Thread the meat and vegetables on the skewers this way: start with a cube of meat; add a tomato wedge, a green pepper square, then a cube of meat, and so on, dividing the ingredients equally among the four skewers.
9. Broil the meat and vegetables on the skewers for 10 minutes. Using a potholder, turn the skewers every few minutes so that the meat can brown on all sides. (You might want to ask an adult to help you with this.)
10. If you grill the kebabs outdoors and the fire is very hot, cook them for less time. Cooked kebabs should be brown on the outside and slightly pink on the inside.

VARIATION: Use any other ingredients you have on hand or that are in season, such as cubes of eggplant, strips of onion, strips of bacon, or whole mushrooms.

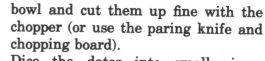

From
ISRAEL
HOLIDAY DATE BITS
Makes about 24 pieces ♨♨♨

The date palm tree grows mainly in desert lands. When the sweet rich dates are ripe, they droop from the tree in heavy bunches. The clusters look like fingers. In fact, the word *date* comes from the Latin word for finger.

In Israel, dates are popular at holiday time, especially during the fall harvest feast, *Succot.* Then dates, berries, figs, and other fruits of the harvest season are used for special desserts.

INGREDIENTS

¾ cup shelled
    walnuts
1   8-oz. pkg. dates
2   or 3 oranges
1¼ cup flour
1¼ t. baking powder
¼ t. salt
2   eggs
½ cup light brown
    sugar, firmly
    packed
¼ cup white sugar
1   or 2 t. butter

EQUIPMENT

measuring cups   sifter
chopper   piece of waxed paper
small wooden bowl   mixing bowl
paring knife   fork
chopping board   mixing spoon
grater   saucepan
juicer   8-in.-square baking
measuring spoons   pan

HOW TO MAKE:

1. Preheat the oven to 325°.
2. Measure the walnuts into a small

bowl and cut them up fine with the chopper (or use the paring knife and chopping board).
3. Dice the dates into small pieces about the size of a pea, using the paring knife and chopping board.
4. Grate the rind from 2 or 3 oranges, using the medium surface of the grater.
5. Slice one of the grated oranges in half and squeeze out 2 tablespoons of orange juice. (The other oranges are still good. Keep them for another use.)
6. Measure the flour, baking powder, and salt and sift them onto the waxed paper.
7. In the mixing bowl, beat the eggs with the fork.
8. Slowly add the sugar (both kinds), stirring the mixture steadily with the spoon.
9. Put the butter in the saucepan to melt over low heat.
10. Add the melted butter to the mixture. Pour in the orange juice. Stir.
11. Add the orange rind, chopped nuts, and dates to the mixture. Then add the flour, salt, and baking powder. Mix well.
12. Grease the 8-in.-square cake pan.
13. Pour the mixture into the pan. Spread it evenly with the back of the spoon.
14. Bake the Date Bits for 40 minutes.
15. Remove the pan from the oven and let cool for 1 hour.
16. Cut the bits into 1-inch-square pieces.

The Egyptians have grown and eaten refreshing cucumbers since biblical times. They were often served with yogurt, another ancient food.

To make yogurt, milk was put in a clay pot, covered with a sack, and left in the sun to thicken and ferment. Today our yogurt is produced by slightly different methods, but it tastes much the same as yogurt always has.

In Egypt, nourishing yogurt is eaten plain, with honey or fruit, or combined with cucumbers to make a cooling salad with a past.

INGREDIENTS

1	large cucumber	2 t. lemon juice
1	cup (½ pt.) plain yogurt	dash of salt and pepper
1	t. dill	3 sprigs fresh mint (if available)

EQUIPMENT

paring knife (or vegetable peeler)
measuring cup
measuring spoons

medium mixing bowl
mixing spoon
serving bowl

HOW TO MAKE:

1. Peel the cucumber and dice it.
2. Put the cucumber, yogurt, dill, and lemon juice into the mixing bowl and stir until well mixed.
3. Season the mixture to your taste with salt and pepper. Place it in the serving bowl.
4. Top it with fresh chopped mint (if available)—do not use dried mint.
5. Cover it with plastic wrap and chill it for 10 minutes in the refrigerator or until you are ready to serve it.

VARIATION: You might also want to mix in 3 tablespoons of chopped walnuts and 3 tablespoons of seedless raisins.

From

INDIA

KAJU (KAH-jew)—Cashew Snack

Serves 4 ♦

Kebabs, curries, and chutneys are specialties of India. But Indian cookery varies so much from region to region and from cook to cook that it isn't easy to find one food that is made and enjoyed in the same way by all the people of India. We did find one, however: nut snacks.

Indians roast their own nuts. After preparing the nuts this way, you might mix them in a bowl with raisins. This makes a healthful Indian-style snack.

NOTE: Almonds, peanuts, pistachio nuts, and other raw nuts can be prepared this way, too. (If you can't find some of these nuts in the supermarket, try a health-food store.)

INGREDIENTS

1½ T. vegetable oil
½ lb. (2 cups) shelled raw unsalted cashews

1 t. salt
dash of cayenne pepper (optional)

EQUIPMENT

measuring spoons
large frying pan
measuring cup
spatula

paper towels
mixing bowl
mixing spoon
serving bowl or dish

HOW TO MAKE:

1. Measure the oil and put it in the frying pan to heat for half a minute.
2. Add the nuts and sauté them in the oil for three minutes, turning them over and over with the spatula.
3. Remove the nuts and put them to drain on the sheets of paper towel, patting them with the toweling to remove any extra oil.
4. In the mixing bowl, combine the salt and pepper.
5. Put the nuts into the bowl and toss them with the spoon, or your hands, until they are coated with the seasoning.
6. Serve the nuts in an attractive bowl or dish.

From
SRI LANKA

KIRIBATH (keer-ee-ʙᴀʜ)—
Rice Squares

Makes 12 pieces ♟♟

Drums beat. A bright festival begins. It is holiday time in Sri Lanka, a sunny island near India. People are dressed in bright silk clothes. Families at home sit around blazing fires. Everyone makes New Year's wishes, hopes for a good harvest in the coming year, and shares tasty squares of *kiribath*.

Rice is the main crop on Sri Lanka, as it is of many Asian nations. It is served with many dishes; so is coconut. *Kiribath* uses both. In Sri Lanka it's made with white rice, but it can be made with brown rice too.

INGREDIENTS

½ cup rice
1½ cups cold water
½ cup flaked
   coconut

2 T. sugar
   fruit jam or
   honey

EQUIPMENT

measuring cups
medium saucepan
  and lid
strainer
small bowl

mixing spoon
shallow baking pan
paring knife
serving plate

HOW TO MAKE:

1. Measure the rice and put it in the saucepan.
2. Wash the rice by adding enough water to cover it and swishing the rice around with your fingers until the water turns cloudy. Then pour off the water. Be careful not to lose any rice. (Using a strainer helps.)
3. Pour the 1½ cups of water over the rice. Cover the saucepan.
4. Bring the rice to a boil over high heat. Turn the heat down.
5. Let the rice cook for about 8 minutes, until it is just tender. If you're using brown rice, it will take longer—about 15 minutes. (The best way to tell if the rice is tender is to take a few grains out of the boiling water, drop them in cold water and then bite on them.) Some of the water will still remain in the saucepan when the rice is tender and the mixture will look soupy.
6. Drain the rice in the strainer and catch the cooking water in a measuring cup. Add enough cold water to make 1 cup.
7. Dump the rice into the saucepan. Refill the saucepan with the measured cup of water.
8. Add the coconut to the water and stir.
9. Let the rice and coconut cook uncovered over a low heat until all the water is gone.
10. Remove the pan from the heat. Pour the rice mixture into the baking pan and smooth it out with a spoon. Sprinkle it with the sugar.
11. Let the mixture cool for 20 minutes. Then put it in the refrigerator for 1 hour.
12. Cut it into squares with the knife.
13. Top each square with fruit jam or honey.
14. Serve it on a colorful plate.

INDONESIA

ATJAR KETIMOEN (AHT-char
KEHT-ee-munh)—Cucumber Relish
Serves 6

Many Indonesian foods are hot with spices, but one sort—*atjar*—is cool. *Atjar* means relish. It's a cooling must at any spicy Indonesian dinner.

Indonesians serve relish along with the main dish in order to cool the tongue between mouthfuls.

Most relishes are mild, like these cucumber slices. They can be made in advance and stored, and if you have leftovers, they'll taste even better the next day.

INGREDIENTS

½	cup water	1	large cucumber
2	t. white vinegar		dash of red
1	t. salt		pepper (optional)

EQUIPMENT

medium mixing bowl   measuring spoon
paring knife   toothpicks (optional)
measuring cup

HOW TO MAKE:

1. Place the water, vinegar, and salt in the bowl.
2. Peel the cucumber. Cut it crosswise into slices about ⅛ inch thick.
3. Float the cucumber slices in the water, vinegar, and salt.
4. Sprinkle the cucumber slices with red pepper.
5. Chill 30 minutes before serving.
6. Eat the cucumber with toothpicks or with your fingers right from the bowl.

41

When a Thai boy or girl is hungry, he or she says, "*Hiu khao.*" This means "I'm hungry for *rice*." In Thai language the word for rice and food is the same, *khao*.

Rice is the most important food in the Thai diet. It's eaten in some form at every meal. Usually the cook prepares more rice than is needed. The leftover rice is served as *khao phat* (fried rice).

Next time you're hungry, say it in Thai —"*Hiu khao.*" Then make some Fried Rice—with shrimp for a hearty main course, or plain as an accompaniment to meat or chicken or fish.

INGREDIENTS

5	scallions	2	t. ginger
3	T. butter	½	t. garlic powder
1	6-oz. can tiny cleaned shrimp	½	t. ground cloves
		1	t. salt
2	cups cooked rice (see next column)	½	t. pepper
		2	T. soy sauce
		2	eggs

EQUIPMENT

paring knife   spatula
measuring spoons   small bowl
large frying pan   fork

HOW TO MAKE:

1. Cut up the scallions—both the white *and* green parts—into small pieces.
2. Melt the butter in the large frying pan over low heat.
3. Sauté the scallions in the frying pan, turning them constantly with the metal spatula until they are golden.
4. Add the drained cooked shrimp to the frying pan. Cook the shrimp for 2 minutes as you cooked the scallions in step 3.
5. Add the cooked rice to the shrimp and scallions. (See next column for directions to cook rice.) Cook it for one minute more. Keep turning the food over and over with the spatula until all the sides are done.
6. Add the ginger, garlic powder, ground cloves, salt, pepper, and soy sauce to the rice, shrimp, and scallions. Stir to combine everything.
7. Crack the eggs into the small bowl. Beat them lightly with the fork.
8. Pour the eggs over the mixture in the frying pan. Turn all ingredients with the spatula for 30 seconds more. Serve.

How to Cook Rice:
INGREDIENTS

1   cup long-grained white rice (makes 2 cups cooked)   1¾ cups cold water

EQUIPMENT

measuring cup   medium saucepan and lid
                                        fork

HOW TO MAKE:

1. Place the rice in the saucepan. Add enough water to cover. Swish the rice with your fingers until the water turns cloudy. Then pour off the water. Be careful not to lose any rice.
2. Pour the 1¾ cups cold water into the saucepan.
3. Bring the water and rice to a boil. Be careful it doesn't boil over.
4. Cover the pan and turn the heat down very low.
5. Let the rice cook for 20 minutes. (After 15 minutes, check to be sure the rice isn't too dry.)
6. Turn off the heat but leave the lid on. (The water should be gone.)
7. Let the rice steam for five more minutes.
8. Fluff the rice with the fork.

Watch an egg turn into a flower. Chinese cooks say that the cooked shreds of egg afloat in this soup look like flower petals. With a few secrets of Chinese cooking you can make this happen.

One is to have all the ingredients out, measured, and ready to use *before* you start to cook. Another is to serve food right after cooking. Some foods look and taste better this way. Egg Flower Soup is one—so serve it promptly.

NOTE: You may know this soup by another name—Egg Drop Soup.

INGREDIENTS

1	T. cornstarch	1	t. salt
2	T. cold water	1	t. chopped
1	egg		scallion or
3	cups clear		parsley (optional)
	canned chicken		
	broth		

EQUIPMENT

measuring spoons	medium saucepan
2 small bowls	mixing spoon
fork	soup bowls

HOW TO MAKE:

1. Put the cornstarch into one of the small bowls and gradually add the water, stirring it with the fork until you no longer see any lumps.
2. Break the egg into the other small bowl and beat it with the fork.
3. Pour the broth into the saucepan. Bring it to a boil over high heat.
4. Add the salt.
5. Give the cornstarch-and-water mixture a quick stir with the fork. Add it to the soup.
6. Stir the soup with the spoon until it thickens and becomes clear—about one minute.
7. Slowly pour the beaten egg into the soup. The egg will cook in the hot soup and form shreds.
8. When all the egg has been added, stir once. Turn off the heat.
9. Pour the soup into four soup bowls. Top the soup with the chopped scallion or parsley for decoration.
10. Pick up the bowl with both hands and sip the soup or eat it with a spoon.

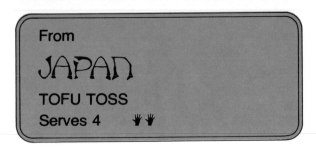

From

JAPAN

TOFU TOSS

Serves 4　♛♛

Tofu is also called bean-curd cake. It's made from dried white soybeans, which have been ground up and jelled. Tofu is sold in small squares that look and feel like custard.

In Japanese cooking, tofu is often mixed with vegetables. Sometimes it's cooked with fish, meat, or soup. The Japanese and Chinese eat soybean in many forms because it's rich in protein. (One form you may have eaten it in is *shoyu*, or soy sauce.)

If you live in a city where you can buy tofu—fresh, dried, or in cans—you can get to know this mild-flavored food.

INGREDIENTS

1	15-oz. can green beans (or 1 lb. of cooked fresh green beans)
2	T. sesame seeds

1	t. sugar
	pinch salt
1	2-in. cake or ½ of a 4-in. cake of tofu (bean curd)

EQUIPMENT

measuring spoons	small bowl
frying pan	medium mixing bowl
spatula	spoon
spoon	serving bowl

HOW TO MAKE:

1. Drain the beans and chill them in the refrigerator.
2. Toast the sesame seeds in the frying pan. To toast: put the frying pan on medium heat; after a minute, add the sesame seeds; turn the seeds over and over with the spatula until they are brown. It will take about 2 minutes.
3. Spoon the sesame seeds into the small bowl. Let them cool.
4. Crumble the seeds between your fingers.
5. Add the sugar and salt to the seeds.
6. Put the tofu into the medium bowl. (Carefully drain off any liquid first since tofu is very soft and breaks easily.) Add the sugar, salt, and seed mixture.
7. Using the spoon, mix and mash the ingredients together.
8. Place the cold string beans in the serving bowl.
9. Spoon the tofu-sesame mixture over the beans. Toss the beans lightly with the spoon.

VARIATION: Instead of the green beans, you might use cooked spinach leaves, bean sprouts, grated raw carrots or sliced raw cucumbers.

44

INTERNATIONAL MENUS

When you're using several recipes, be sure to check and see the amount each recipe makes. Some recipes may have to be doubled, so that there will be enough to go around.

Surprise Weekend Brunch

A late meal in pajamas and slippers can be a nice change on Saturday or Sunday. Make this brunch when friends spend the night—or serve it to surprise your family.

Fruit Juice
Rabanadas or Sirniki
Breakfast Cocoa

Family Celebration Dinner

These are for a many-course dinner. Make some or all of them for a birthday, anniversary, or first-day-of-summer feast. Add color to your celebration by decorating the table with a bowl of flowers or leaves.

Egg Flower Soup
Golden Fried Rice
Summer Salads
Early American Graham Cracker Cake

After-School Get-Together

Invite people to your house to cook as well as to eat. Everyone can help make the snacks on this menu.

Kaju
Citrus Pops or Maple Snow
Tea and Sugar Crisps

International Costume Fete

Ask your guests to dress in costumes from other countries. Look for international games to play and songs to sing.

Guacamole
Prawns
Cornbread
Spinach Pie
Chocolate Torte

African Lunch

Combine foods from the continent of Africa for a hearty lunch.

Groundnut Soup
Fufu
Fruit Platter

CSM

Meat, fish, eggs, milk, beans, nuts—these are high-protein foods. Many are used in the recipes in this book. But some people don't have diets rich in protein. That is because high-protein foods are expensive and not always easily available. Droughts or floods can destroy a country's crops for a year or more. So scientists must search for new supplies of protein.

One food that was developed in the 1960's is CSM. CSM is a precooked powder made of cornmeal, soy flour, and nonfat dry milk, plus vitamins and minerals. The supply of CSM depends on crop surpluses. It isn't always available. But when it is, CSM is an important addition to diets poor in protein.

Today the United States government, UNICEF, and other agencies distribute CSM in more than a hundred countries. The bland taste makes it easy to add to many national foods without changing their taste. For example, in Colombia, CSM can be added to tortillas and turnovers. In India, it's put into porridge and snacks. In West Africa, stews are made with CSM.

Here are two simple recipes using CSM. The Vegetable Soup serves a crowd. So does the Banana Cake (an Indonesian favorite).

You can get more information about CSM and how UNICEF distributes it by writing to the U.S. Committee for UNICEF. They also will send you a sample of CSM when it's available.

The U.S. Committee for UNICEF
331 East 38 Street
New York, New York 10016

Ingredients

1 onion
3 or 4 raw carrots
2 or 3 stalks celery
2 potatoes
2 or 3 tomatoes
1 small head of cabbage, or ¼ lb. spinach, or other green vegetable

½ cup vegetable oil, butter, or other fat
3 qt. water
1 t. or more salt
½ t. or more pepper
1 cup CSM
2 cups *cold* water

Equipment

paring knife
cutting board
large stewing pot with lid, or Dutch oven and lid
mixing spoon

measuring cups
peeler

measuring spoons

How to Make:

1. Peel and slice the onion.
2. Slice the carrots into ¼-in. pieces until you have 1 cup.
3. Slice the celery in the same way until you have 1 cup.
4. Peel and cut the potatoes into bite-sized pieces until you have 2 cups.
5. Cut up enough tomatoes to measure 2 cups.
6. Coarsely chop enough cabbage (or spinach or other vegetable) to measure 2 cups.

7. Put the vegetable oil (or fat) in the stewing pot. Add the onions, carrots, celery, and potatoes.
8. Cook over low heat for 10 minutes—the mixture should gently simmer—stirring occasionally with a spoon.
9. Add the tomatoes and cook another 5 minutes, stirring occasionally.
10. Add the water, salt, and pepper. Turn the heat up to medium and bring to a boil.
11. When boiling, add the cabbage or spinach.
12. Cover and simmer about 20 minutes until the vegetables are tender.
13. Mix the CSM with the 2 cups of cold water and stir into the simmering liquid.
14. Bring the soup again to the boil and cook for 5 to 10 more minutes.

VARIATIONS: Any vegetables may be used, including red or green peppers, squash, green leafy vegetables, okra, green peas, and green beans.

In some parts of Latin American, sections of corn on the cob and slices of plantain, and cassava or yucca are added. Green herbs, such as parsley and chives, may also be used for additional flavor.

CSM Recipe

Banana Cake
Makes 20 to 30 pieces

Ingredients

1 cup soft margarine (2 sticks)

1½ cups sugar
4 eggs
4 or 5 bananas (2 cups mashed)
3 cups CSM
2 t. baking powder
1 or 2 t. margarine

Equipment

measuring cups	medium mixing bowl
measuring spoons	kitchen fork
large mixing bowl	2 8-in. cake pans or
mixing spoon	1 large cake pan
small dish	

How to Make:

1. Preheat oven to 375°.
2. Measure out the margarine and sugar, put them into the large mixing bowl, and beat until well combined.
3. Add the eggs one at a time. First crack the egg into a small dish. Then pour it into the mixing bowl. Beat after each egg is added.
4. Peel the bananas and mash them with a fork in the medium mixing bowl. You should have 2 cups of mashed banana.
5. Add the 3 cups of CSM and the 2 teaspoons of baking powder to the ingredients in the large mixing bowl.
6. Stir in the mashed bananas and mix thoroughly.
7. Grease the cake pan or pans with the 1 or 2 teaspoons of margarine.
8. Pour the mixture into the pan or pans and spread evenly with the back of a spoon.
9. Put in the oven and bake at 375° for 45 minutes. Test for doneness with a toothpick. If the cake isn't done, bake for 5 minutes longer.

GLOSSARY OF ILLUSTRATIONS

CANADA, page 1. In Canada, a spring sleigh ride calls for a wool neck scarf, heavy lumberjack cap, and a warm fur-lined coat.

PUERTO RICO, page 3. Her costume is modeled on an early colonial dress brought from Spain. The dress is worn for celebrations of Epiphany, or Three Kings' Day.

MEXICO, page 4. The girl is wearing a traditional dress of the Puebla region called the *china poblana.* The boy wears a wool *serape* over his white shirt and pants.

HAITI, page 5. The hat, cotton shawl, and dress are a Haitian freed woman's costume, worn in honor of the winning of freedom from slavery.

BARBADOS, page 6. This West Indian skirt and matching kerchief are of madras plaid, popular in the West Indies.

VENEZUELA, page 7. These costumes are worn for the folklore festival in San Fernando de Apure in Venezuela. The boy wears a wide-brimmed hat, called *sombrero de pelo de guama,* which is made from fibers of the fruit of the guama tree. A wool *ruana* covers his white shirt and pants. The girl has on a cotton skirt and a cape made of wool.

PERU, page 9. A striped wool *poncho* and a broad hat called a *montera* is the way Quechua Indians from Cuzco, Peru, dress.

BRAZIL, page 11. Brazilian ranchers wear sturdy pants called *bombachas,* suited to horseback riding in rough country.

MOROCCO, page 12. This bright wool robe is called a *djellaba* and the patterned cap is a *tagia.*

GHANA, Page 13. The printed toga the Ashanti boy is wearing is made of *kente* cloth, used on ceremonial costumes.

NIGERIA, page 15. A special occasion in Nigeria calls for a head tie called a *gele,* a blouse called a *buba,* and a wrap-around skirt called an *irobirin,* held by a sash called an *iborun.* The clothes are Yoruba.

CAMEROON, page 16. The pants and hat and the boat are commonly found in the Lake Chad region of Cameroon. The boy is dreaming of fishing off the coast for luscious prawns.

ZAIRE, page 17. Young girls in Zaire often wear their hair in elaborate braided styles. The red and orange dress is of the kind usually worn on holidays and special visits.

UGANDA, page 18. A girl from the Luo tribe wears a bark-cloth cape draped over her right shoulder and many silver necklaces.

ICELAND, page 19. An Icelandic girl's hat is called a *hufá,* or *hupá,* and is a symbol of good fortune. Both the boy and the girl are wearing folk costumes.

PORTUGAL, page 20. A Portuguese shepherd boy wears a traditional knitted cap. His costume is decorated with bright buttons.

IRELAND, page 22. The sleeveless sweater, worn over a shirt, and the cap are everyday dress for cool weather in Ireland.

FRANCE, page 23. On top of the girl's head is a large stiff bow that looks almost like a hat. This headdress is part of the costume worn in Alsace, a province of France.

BELGIUM, page 24. The girl is wearing a Belgian folk costume.

HOLLAND, page 25. Stiff petticoats are worn under these dresses from the village of Volendam in Holland.

GERMANY, page 26. Typical dress in Bavaria (in Southern Germany) is leather pants called *lederhosen* and a felt hat.

SWEDEN, page 27. This Swedish boy is dressed as a historical Viking.

FINLAND, page 29. The pointed shoes of this Lapp boy are called *mutukas.* He wears a tunic and trousers made from blue dyed reindeer skin.

POLAND, page 30. The starched white hat, with ribbons down the back is still worn by girls from some of the old traditional families in the Lowicz part of Poland.

HUNGARY, page 31. The boy and girl are in Sunday dress. The boy's white linen shirt has bands of lace. His tall hat is felt, and his vest is embroidered. The girl's dress is from the northern part of Hungary.

ITALY, page 32. The early Roman is wearing a *toga.*

GREECE, page 33. A farmer's daughter from near Florina wears a black tunic over her white linen chemise. The way she has folded and tied her scarf tells what village she is from.

RUSSIA, page 34. The cold winters in the Asian part of the Soviet Union call for a fox-fur cap and high boots.

ISRAEL, page 37. Yemenite women and girls wear dresses like these, decorated with fine embroidery.

EGYPT, page 38. The Egyptian boy wears a striped *galabiya* and a skullcap.

INDIA, page 39. A graceful *sari* and a short blouse called a *choli* make up this Indian girl's everyday dress. The unusual fruits she is picking are cashew fruits—the nuts grow at the bottom of the fruit.

SRI LANKA, page 40. Everyday dress in Sri Lanka includes a turban.

INDONESIA, page 41. Unusually shaped headdresses top the delicate Indonesian holiday costumes. The skirt is called a *kain.* The long sleeved blouse is a *kebaya.*

CHINA, page 43. The Chinese children are wearing everyday cotton jackets and pants.

JAPAN, page 44. The cook is wearing a *kimono,* held together by a colorful sash called an *obi.*

METRIC AND U.S. MEASURES

The system of measurement used in the United States is different from the metric system most countries use. (The British use still a third system.) In the U.S. the liquid measure of one cup is used to measure both liquid and dry ingredients. The metric system measures dry ingredients by weight (grams and kilograms) and liquids by centimeters, liters, and milliliters. This difference makes it hard to convert from U.S. to metric measures with complete accuracy. However, listed here are some U.S. measures and their approximate metric equivalents.

LIQUID MEASURE

U.S.	Metric
1 teaspoon	5 cubic centimeters
1 tablespoon	15 cubic centimeters
1 ounce	30 milliliters
1 cup	about ¼ liter
1 quart	about 1 liter

(Remember, there are 8 ounces in one U.S. cup and 32 ounces in one quart.)

DRY MEASURE

U.S.	Metric
1 ounce	about 28 grams
1 pound	about 454 grams

(Remember, there are 16 ounces in a U.S. pound.)

SOME BASIC FOODS

butter	1 tablespoon =	15 grams
	½ cup =	125 grams
flour	¼ cup =	35 grams
	1 cup =	140 grams
rice	1 cup =	240 grams
salt	1 tablespoon =	15 grams
spices (ground)	1 teaspoon =	2½ grams
sugar	1 tablespoon =	15 grams
	1 cup =	240 grams

INDEX